Original title:
Rooms of My Life

Copyright © 2025 Creative Arts Management OÜ
All rights reserved.

Author: Gideon Barrett
ISBN HARDBACK: 978-1-80587-054-8
ISBN PAPERBACK: 978-1-80587-524-6

The Spirit of Each Space

In the kitchen, pots clank loud,
Spicy scents dance, a savory crowd.
The chair squeaks tales of last night's feast,
While crumbs plot for a sneaky beast.

The hallway whispers of shoes in a mess,
Chasing the pets, causing distress.
Battery-operated cars zoom by,
Watch out! Here comes a sticky pie!

Traces of Laughter in the Air

In the bedroom, socks form a line,
Worn out from dances, they'll be just fine.
The blanket fort hides secrets untold,
Where whispers and dreams boldly unfold.

The bathroom echoes with funny tunes,
As rubber ducks plot underwater runes.
Who knew shampoo bottles could sing?
This tiled stage makes the toothbrush swing!

Secret Nooks and Crannies

Under the stairs, a map of old dreams,
Dust bunnies giggle in hidden themes.
The cupboard's a lair for treasures galore,
Where leftover snacks loom, begging for more.

Behind the curtains, the cat strikes a pose,
Prowling for mischief, she strikes little blows.
A world of socks, forgotten and wild,
Even the vacuum cleaner's beguiled!

Reflections in the Dusty Glass

On the table, a mirror of messy cheer,
Coffee rings tell tales of adventure near.
Fingerprints smudge the tales we've spun,
Each one a quirk, a laugh, and some fun.

The window frames scenes of life outside,
Where rain drops giggle, swirling with pride.
The world keeps turning, but here we stay,
In the calm of our chaos, we find our play.

Beyond Closed Doors

Behind the door, who knows what's there?
A sock on the floor and a comical stare.
Dust bunnies dance like they're on parade,
While my vacuum hides, plotting its escape.

A fridge that sings, oh, what a tune!
Leftovers lurking beneath the moon.
Each creak of the floor, a chatty old friend,
Whispering secrets that never quite end.

Dialogues with the Past

I found an old diary, locked in a drawer,
Each entry I read made me laugh even more.
Cringe-worthy crushes, such youthful despair,
I was convinced that the world wasn't fair.

In an ancient photo, my hair is a fright,
I wore neon leg warmers that glowed in the night.
Oh, how I'd strut on a dance floor with glee,
Only to trip on my own two left feet!

The Weight of Memories

Old toys are stacked like a tower so high,
A testament to times that just zoomed by.
Action figures muse on their battles of yore,
While board games plot to be played once more.

Photos of family with faces so round,
Caught in the act of goofiness found.
Grandpa's wild wig and Auntie's big grin,
Those snapshots of joy, where do I begin?

A Corner of Peace

In a corner, I found my favorite chair,
Where I can daydream without a care.
Books stacked high, like a wobbly tower,
Each story whispers, lending me power.

With a cup of tea, I settle in tight,
While cushions conspire to hold me just right.
The outside world fades, with its hustle and fuss,
And here in my nook, I just laugh at the bus!

The Echo Chamber of Dreams

In the corner, a sock glares bright,
Hoping to end its lone, sad plight.
A rubber duck floats, lost in thought,
Dreaming of battles it never fought.

The clock ticks in sync with my snore,
Counting sheep with a mustache galore.
Laughter bounces off the wallpaper,
Whispers of joy in this fun escape.

A cereal box wins a gold medal,
In a race of crumbs that never settle.
Chairs gossip about the days gone by,
Tickling secrets that make me sigh.

Like stage props in this odd play,
Each has a role, come what may.
I slip on a banana peel o' dreams,
In a world where everything gleams.

Fragments of Yesteryears

Old photographs gather dust,
Smiling faces show their trust.
In a drawer, memories jive,
Ignoring the rules of 'stay alive.'

A broken toy lays down the law,
In a funk, it's a silent awe.
Shirts from the past chat away,
While mismatched socks decide to play.

Dust bunnies stage a fun parade,
Curious as they begin to invade.
Recipes failed in their wild quest,
Create a dish that looks like a pest.

Each crack in the wall whispers cheers,
Celebrating the dance of the years.
All that glitters may not be gold,
But laughter remains, ancient and bold.

Lanterns in the Night

The night-light flickers a silly dance,
Bugs get lost in a wallflower trance.
Shadows giggle, pulling my leg,
While the cat plans a ninja's peg.

Outside, the moon pretends to glow,
Hiding behind clouds in a cheeky show.
Twinkling stars drop jokes of their own,
Read them like texts on a funky phone.

A ghost in the corner takes a bow,
Telling tales to the sleepy cow.
Ghostly giggles fill the room,
With a squeaky floor as a boom.

Pillows stash dreams, vibrant and bright,
Making mischief in the middle of night.
Lanterns blink with laughter and cheer,
Hiding my wishes, but always near.

Stories Carved into the Furniture

The chair creaks as secrets unfold,
Whispers of mischief, daring and bold.
A table bears the stains of cheer,
Replaying feasts from yesteryear.

A couch thinks it's a throne of grace,
Hosting popcorn fights in a furry embrace.
The lamp juggles shadows and light,
Throwing a dance in the heart of the night.

Old books lie down with a yawn,
Hatching stories till the early dawn.
The dresser giggles as it folds,
Map of memories, untold and old.

Plates with chips laugh in delight,
Chasing crumbs in a hilarious flight.
Every piece of this playful array,
Shares a tale of the goofy day.

Faded Photographs

Hanging on the wall with style,
A picture of me wearing no smile.
My hair was big, my shirt was bright,
I still don't know why I chose that night.

My friends all pose, with thumbs up high,
An awkward crew, oh me, oh my!
Those Puerto Rican shirts and flip-flop shoes,
Fashion advice I sadly refuse.

Each photo tells a tale untrue,
Of wild adventures—none I knew.
A dorky laugh, a silly face,
I'm forever trapped in this time and space.

Yet in the blur, some joy does gleam,
My faded past, a funny dream.
As laughter echoes, the years roll by,
I cherish these moments with a sigh.

Mirrors of Regret

In the hallway stands a glass so clear,
Reflecting me, full of cheer.
But when I glance, what do I see?
A face that laughs, then sighs at me.

Staring back with wild surprise,
A prankster grin and squinty eyes.
Did I really wear that shirt today?
Oh, mirrors, why must you betray?

I pose like a star in my own show,
The mirror laughs as I strike a faux.
"Who's that?" I ask, with a wink so sly,
The glass just giggles while I comply.

Though I regret some choices made,
I can't deny these memories played.
Every wrinkle laughs a story loud,
In this crazy life, I'm forever proud.

The Symphony of Silence

In the quiet hour of the night,
I hear the oddest noise take flight.
A creak, a thump, a ghostly moan,
Or maybe it's just the cat alone?

Balloons in the corner, still inflated,
They mock me—uninvited, uncreated.
Dancing shadows on the wall,
Here's my silent, unscripted hall!

The clock ticks slow, a drumbeat weird,
Echoes of laughter I once cheered.
Nonsense serenades fill the air,
While socks and toys lounge everywhere.

This symphony plays in joyful strife,
Notes of mess in the chaos of life.
Trapped in this concert, I must confess,
Sometimes silence screams, just to impress.

Footprints on the Floor

Tiny prints scattered all around,
A maze of mischief on the ground.
Chocolate smears from yesterday's fun,
Who knew mischief could weigh a ton?

Wobbly tracks from muddy shoes,
Leading to snacks and snooze-filled snooze.
Mom's on the hunt with a mop in hand,
Trying to figure out our wild plan.

Each step reveals a story bright,
Of silly chases in broad daylight.
Guess who's hiding behind the door?
The ultimate trickster on the floor!

So we dance through life, make such a mess,
Every footprint is a tale to express.
Laughter echoes as we know it's true,
These silly moments will pull us through.

Warmth of Familiarity.

In the kitchen, pots and pans sing,
A dance of chaos, a culinary fling.
Spices leap from their jars in jest,
Mismatched socks hide, it's quite the mess.

The living room's a sofa dive,
With crumbs and pillows that thrive.
Laughter bounces from wall to wall,
The dog on the couch claims it all.

In the bathroom, bubbles take flight,
Rubber ducks float, oh what a sight!
Suds whisper secrets as they confide,
While I trip on towels left aside.

Upstairs in the office, chaos reigns,
Paper mountains and caffeine stains.
The cat has claimed the keyboard, too,
Typing tales of slippers and a shoe.

Echoes in Every Corner

In the hall, shoes face the wall,
A mismatched army ready to fall.
They've stories to tell of every wander,
Of adventures lost in their ponder.

The closet giggles, what a sight,
Dresses whisper, 'Wear us tonight!'
Hats chat about the places they've been,
While dust bunnies play hide and seek unseen.

The attic sings with memories old,
Boxes of treasures and stories untold.
There's a strange doll that winks, oh dear!
Fred the stuffed bear still holds my beer!

In the cellar, the snacks form a pact,
Chips and dips form their snacking act.
"They'll never find us," the cheese puffs boast,
While soda cans cheer for their fizzing toast.

Shadows of Forgotten Days

In the corner of my mind, shadows play,
Old toys and memories in disarray.
There's a teddy bear who lost its fluff,
Complaining daily, 'I've had enough!'

A calendar hangs, pages all torn,
Dates forgotten, like leaves they've worn.
It sighs, 'I've stood here year upon year,
Watching you live, sometimes in fear!'

The old clock groans, seconds move slow,
'Is this what they mean by time on the go?'
It ticks and tocks, plotting its plan,
To snatch back moments since time began.

The dust gathers low, a silent brigade,
With a mission of whispers in the glade.
'We'll catch those laughs, and frame them just right,
In the scrapbook of folly, a funny delight!'

The Shelves of Memory

On the shelves, books stand at ease,
Spilling secrets with a gentle breeze.
They argue softly, 'Who's the best?'
While one falls down, claiming a rest.

Candles flicker with stories to share,
Of birthdays and parties, all held with flair.
A melted one grumbles, 'Why am I here?'
'To light up our smiles, my dear, my dear!'

In the corner, a vase starts to hum,
'Fill me with flowers, don't let them glum!'
But the plastic ones giggle, "We're here for the fun!"
A party of colors, they twirl in the sun.

The memories sit, a quirky parade,
In this gallery oddity, laughter's displayed.
Each trinket, a tale of ongoing delight,
In the strange exhibit of day and night.

The Canvas of Sorrow

In every corner, a portrait hangs,
Whispers of laughter mixed with clangs.
I tripped on a memory, face first in paint,
Giggling at colors that all seem quaint.

A brushstroke of chaos, a splash of cheer,
The muse is a cat, not quite sincere.
She sneezes confetti, with a flick of her tail,
While I clean the mess—oh, what a tale!

Yet under the shadows, a smile will creep,
For every flop is a promise we keep.
In this gallery wild, life paints its own way,
Where even the blunders make room for play.

A Staircase of Hope

A staircase wobbles, creaks with delight,
Each step is a giggle, a comedic sight.
I climb with ambition, but trip on a shoe,
Rolling down laughter, who knew it was you?

With banisters swirling like waltzing stars,
I ponder my future while dodging bizarre.
What if I tumble, what if I fly?
A bounce in my step, I won't say goodbye!

The higher I go, the funnier it gets,
With each shaky stair, I defy all my debts.
A summit of chuckles, I reach for the top,
Where hope meets hilarity, and never will stop.

The Parlor of Dreams

In a parlor where whimsy dances on air,
I sip on my tea while floating, I swear.
The chairs tell me secrets, the curtains conspire,
Whispers of nonsense that lift my heart higher.

A rug that can giggle when stepped on with care,
It tickles my toes and zips me from despair.
I try on the hats, each one tells a joke,
Laughter erupts with each quirky stroke.

While the clock spins in circles, my dreams take flight,
Winking and blinking while I laugh through the night.
In this magical space, where silliness beams,
I'll hold on forever to the spirit of dreams.

Hidden Passages

Within hidden passages, laughter runs free,
A door creaks open, jokes spill like tea.
I navigate hallways where quirks come alive,
Each corner a riddle, where giggles contrive.

I found a secret where sock puppets play,
They throw me puns that just brighten the day.
A wardrobe that dances, a closet with flair,
In this maze of humor, I lose all my care.

Peeking through keyholes to worlds full of bliss,
Where even a blush can turn into a kiss.
So here in the nooks, I'll forever reside,
Embracing the funny, with grins open wide.

Celestial Ceilings

Beneath the stars, I lay in bed,
Pondering dreams, where socks are wed.
The popcorn ceiling looks like space,
Where aliens dance in a sock race.

My cat thinks it's her personal sky,
Chasing dust bunnies as they fly.
In this vast universe, I'm a tiny dot,
With a laundry pile that's quite the lot.

A chandelier sways like a disco ball,
Each light flicker gives a silent call.
Mom's old lamp that refuses to die,
Looks down upon my dreams gone awry.

So here I lie with giggles and glee,
In a galaxy made from laundry debris.
The ceiling above, a canvas of cheer,
In my comical cosmos, I persevere.

The Solitude of Solace

In corners where the dust settles thick,
I find solace in that old clock's tick.
It whispers secrets with every chime,
Like a stand-up comic who steals my time.

Socks that vanished into the void,
Leave a trail of laughter, not annoyed.
The chair I bought on a whim and a dare,
Lurks in silence as I comb my hair.

The neighbors' antics inspire my glee,
Fighting over who's more kooky, just me!
Each wall has ears, and they've heard it all,
From soap opera dramas to beer pong calls.

In solitude, a giggle erupts,
Even the goldfish seems to erupt.
My little haven, forever bizarre,
Where solitude lives, wrapped in a jar.

Stairs to Yesterday

Each step I climb feels like a prank,
With squeaks and creaks filling the tank.
These stairs hold stories of slips and falls,
With echoes of giggles bouncing off walls.

I trip over memories, both good and weird,
Like the time my old bike tires disappeared.
Nostalgia swirls in a whimsical dance,
While I fumble up the steps, lost in a trance.

The banister's got a grip like a friend,
Holding me up as I round the bend.
With every footfall, I laugh at the way,
Life's staircase leads me back to play.

At the top, I find a treasure trove,
Dusty old boxes, where stories rove.
I peek inside and chuckle with glee,
Stairs to yesterday, come laugh with me!

The Aroma of Old Pages

In my library, time takes a breath,
The scent of old pages, a whisper of death.
Ink stains from love letters, long gone,
Welcome me back, oh, literary dawn.

I open a book, and giggles appear,
As dust bunnies cling like they're in here.
Each turn of a page a ticklish delight,
As characters dance into the night.

Crusty old plots make my head spin,
Like jam on a donut, a literary win.
I snicker at phrases like 'fainting maid,'
In worlds that promise a better upgrade.

So here I sit, lost in the scheme,
With thoughts of plots like an ice cream dream.
The aroma surrounds, a comforting haze,
In the world of old pages, I laugh for days.

The Ghosts We Host

In the attic, dust bunnies dance,
Ghosts of old toys take their chance.
A pirate ship made of a shoe,
Pillaging echoes, they plan their coup.

In the kitchen, a spatula's sigh,
Claims it wielded the flippering pie.
The fridge whispers secrets of cheese,
Conversations with pickles, oh what a tease!

The living room holds a couch so wise,
Telling tales with its plushy guise.
Dancing slippers, they twirl on their own,
While the TV claims to be in the zone.

Beneath the bed, there's laughter's trace,
Monsters giggling, a cryptic race.
They argue on who will scare the most,
But end up just being quite the host!

Gilded Frames

On the wall, the portraits grin wide,
They mock my fashion with crafty pride.
While I try on hats from yesteryear,
They cluck and they cackle, 'Oh dear, oh dear!'

A picture of Grandma with shades and a grin,
Says I wear my outfits with zero sin.
Uncle Joe in a bow tie so bright,
Thought it was fancy—what a sight!

Each frame holds tales of quirky glee,
Like cousin Ned climbing up a tree.
It's a gallery of goofs and delight,
Where silliness dances and takes flight.

Sometimes I hear them whisper and plot,
How to out-fun me, I've got to be hot.
But I'll repaint the walls with a vibrant hue,
And laugh as they flee from my joy anew!

Patterns of Existence

In the corners, the mismatched socks,
Woven stories of laundry clock.
Each pair a tale, a funny plight,
How they wander, missing their right.

The coffee cups stacked in a pile,
Whispering secrets, provoking a smile.
One claims it's the mug of a hero,
While another just wants to be a zero.

The curtains sway, like dancers at play,
Judging my life from day to day.
They gossip about the sock on the floor,
And ponder if I'll ever clean more.

On the pantry shelves, the cans do rave,
Each with a dream they desperately crave.
To be part of dinner, a feast to parade,
While I just want chips; it's plans that I've laid!

Breezes of Change

A breeze sneaks in through the window's crack,
Whispers of change, there's no looking back.
It ruffles the papers I thought I'd filed,
Turning my chaos into something wild.

The curtains leap, a jubilant cheer,
Conspiring with dust motes, drawing near.
They declare it's time for a room makeover,
But my wallet groans like an old hangover.

The plants start to shimmy, roots out of place,
They're practicing yoga, embracing the space.
Potting soil flings like confetti around,
While I dodge rogue leaves, it's chaos profound!

The fan spins fast, like a whirlwind of fun,
Declaring that life will soon be a run.
So I laugh with the breeze and embrace the change,
Because normal is boring, and that's just plain strange!

Whispers Behind Closed Doors

In the kitchen, pots go clink,
Fridge hums secrets, what do you think?
Behind closed doors, snacks are schemed,
While outside, healthy choices are dreamed.

Laughter echoes from the bathroom stall,
As soap suds rise, they might just fall.
Toothbrushes battle like swords of foam,
Who knew hygiene could feel like home?

In the living room, cushions conspire,
To hide the remote, oh, they conspire!
They're plotting a game of hide and seek,
While I just want to binge-watch next week.

So I trip on shoes left by the door,
Wondering what is life really for?
The walls might giggle, the floorboards sigh,
In these cozy nooks, I just want to fly.

Echoes in the Hallway

Footsteps dance in the echoing hall,
Shadows chase light, having a ball.
A mop sings a tune, who knew it could?
Broomsticks and dust make my day feel good.

Close the door softly, don't wake the cat,
He's plotting mischief, the sly little brat.
Suitcases sigh in the corner so cheap,
Dreaming of travels while I'm fast asleep.

Posters on walls grin, can't take it back,
They've seen every angle, each crazy track.
Reminders of laughter, a snippet of age,
Every corner's a chapter, every wall's a page.

In the hallway, echoes laugh with glee,
Old memories dance, just like a bee.
With a little whimsy and plenty of cheer,
These echoes of life are so very clear.

Shadows of Forgotten Corners

Dust bunnies hide in the corners unseen,
Playing hide and seek like they're on the scene.
Old shoes forgotten, with laces all frayed,
Whisper of adventures that never got made.

Underneath beds, we find what's alive,
A sock, a toy, a 'where'd that come from' vibe.
Shadows flicker, telling stories so grand,
Of nights full of dreams, and sleepovers planned.

The closet's a portal, if you dare to explore,
Coats upon coats, but there's always room for more.
Sweaters that fit in a decade long past,
Each one a memory, a laugh that came fast.

Embrace the oddness that lives in those nooks,
For in the chaos, the best story cooks.
It's a carnival of laughter and fun,
In these shadowy corners, life is never done.

Windows to My Memories

The window squeaks with every small breeze,
Peeking out, it spots the buzzing bees.
Each pane is a portal to times gone by,
Where laughter drifted like clouds in the sky.

Potted plants wave as if to say hi,
Chasing away worries, they flutter and sigh.
Sunlight dances and makes a sweet toast,
To days filled with giggles we miss the most.

Birds perched outside sing their silly tune,
As I reminisce about afternoons in June.
Every glance out, a chapter to see,
Unlocking a door to sweet memories.

So here at the window, life's sketched with glee,
In each laugh and waltz, I find a part of me.
With curtains that flutter, an old-world charm,
These moments forever hold me warm.

Colors of Emotion on the Walls

The yellow is happy, or so I've been told,
But my walls are more red from the ketchup that's bold.
Blue for the days when I think of my socks,
And green for the plants that annoy me in blocks.

I painted one wall with a color called 'shout',
It's a mess when my friends all come round to hang out.
Magenta for laughter, a pink for my cries,
This house is a circus, oh what a surprise!

With stripes that are wobbly and polka dots bright,
I'm lost in a canvas that gives quite a fright.
Each hue tells a story, a blunder, a prank,
At least it's not boring, I'll give it an 'A' rank.

So here is my patchwork, my sanctuary bright,
In the land of my laughter, my walls see the light.
A spectrum of chaos, a kaleidoscope gas,
In this quirky abode, good vibes ever last!

The Library of My Heart

In a corner sits wisdom, in the form of a book,
But it's mostly just mishaps, some clumsiness I took.
Fiction full of blunders and genres so wide,
A memoir of my life, with nonsense inside.

There's a section for love topped with a dust layer,
It's like my old crush, just a tad too fair.
And thrillers make me sweat, they're reads I can't spare,
As characters run wild, you won't find me there!

Comedy is tucked with its giggles and glee,
Where I murmur and chuckle - who just touched the bee?
I've got mysteries stacked on an unstable shelf,
As I trip down the aisles, enjoying myself.

So come take a peak at the tales that I weave,
Just watch where you step, you might take a leave.
In this library of heart, the stories abound,
Enjoy the adventures, where laughter is found!

Paths Worn by Time

Oh, the paths of my youth, they're crooked and spry,
With memories of cycling and almost a fly.
Each stone tells a tale, some silly, some bold,
As I tripped on the way to the ice cream I sold.

There's a route with my dog, who would stop, then he'd run,
Chasing after a squirrel - it was all just good fun.
But the squirrels are wily, they lead me a chase,
While I end up faceplanting, oh what a disgrace!

In the park where I played, my friends formed a line,
But our games of 'tag' often ended in whines.
We'd stomp through the mud, let the laughter collide,
Now the paths bear the footprints of fun and of pride.

With each pebble that's shifted and root that I bump,
These trails that I wander, they happily thump.
A journey of giggles, a map of my glee,
Each stride holds a memory, forever to be!

Conversations with the Ghosts

In the evening, I chat with my shadowy friends,
Who remind me of times when my laughter transcends.
They float with good humor, they joke from the past,
While I sit with my tea, these chats never last.

'Remember that time you tripped over the cat?'
One ghost says with glee, while I laugh at that.
'Or when you mistook that poodle for bread?'
I shudder, I weep, yes, those thoughts fill with dread.

They dance on the ceiling, they sway with delight,
With their tales of my folly, each prank takes flight.
'Oh, don't be so serious, just let yourself go!
Life's funnier here, don't be such a no-show!'

So I chuckle and grin, take a sip from my cup,
With my spectral companions, who never say 'stop.'
In the twilight of laughter, we banter and croon,
These conversations are magic that brighten the gloom!

The Symphony of Solitude

In a quiet nook, I play my tune,
Socks on my hands, I dance with a broom.
The cat looks on, a judging friend,
While I conduct chaos, no need to pretend.

The fridge hums softly, a melody sweet,
With leftover pizza, my favorite treat.
I twirl and I sway, in my grand hall's delight,
A solo performance, under the dim light.

Echoes of laughter, from the halls of my mind,
Where I trip on the rug, blissfully blind.
The walls whisper secrets, that only I hear,
In this symphony of silence, nothing to fear.

So here I reside, with humor in tow,
In my solo concert, I steal the show.
Each quirky note, a reveler's cheer,
In my everyday stage, the audience near.

A Tapestry of Moments

Moments like thread, I weave and I spin,
A breakfast mishap, spaghetti with gin.
The cat steals my toast, with a flick of her tail,
While I search for my phone, in the laundry trail.

Memories tangled, a technicolor mess,
A sock puppet drama, my true claim to success.
Each laugh is a stitch, in my woven delight,
As I craft my own history, quirky but bright.

From birthday cake mishaps, to spontaneous games,
Every moment I'm weaving, a thread that remains.
The quilt of my laughter, the fabric of fun,
In this tapestry rich, my joy's never done.

So here I abide, in colors so bold,
With stories unfurling, and legends retold.
Each moment a blessing, in life's funny loom,
I stitch laughs together, in my cozy room.

Sunbeams in Forgotten Places

In the corner where dust bunnies thrive,
I find the sunbeams that make me feel alive.
A chair with a squeak, it sings to my heart,
While shadows do pirouettes, a playful art.

Under the couch, I unearth a treasure,
A moldy sandwich, my fondness for measure.
It's the quirky finds that tickle my soul,
In forgotten places, I discover my role.

Sunbeams that dance on cobwebs and grime,
Whispering secrets of this silly time.
With each flicker of light, a reason to grin,
In my corners of bliss, where the laughter begins.

So I bask in the glow of these odd little beams,
Creating my happiness, crafting my dreams.
In this riot of sunlight, I play hide and seek,
With the magical moments, where joy's far from meek.

Thresholds of Change

At the doorway of whim, I leap with delight,
Trading chores for a dance in the night.
I trip over shoes, turn errands to fun,
While my to-do list laughs—oh, it weighs a ton!

One step through the threshold, chaos unfolds,
Pajamas by noon, and mischief it molds.
With a wink and a nudge, I tackle the day,
Turning mundane to magic, come what may.

The door swings wide open, with possibilities vast,
I juggle my plans, a comedic contrast.
With each little change, I groove to the beat,
As life keeps on dancing, I shuffle my feet.

So here's to the thresholds, the quirks in my fate,
Where change is a giggle I celebrate.
With laughter as armor, I step into glee,
In this adventure of humor, I'm wild and free.

Traces of Laughter

In the corner, socks once paired,
Now just one sits, soul bared.
Jokes about where it might roam,
Perhaps it's set off to find a home.

The fridge holds treasures, moldy and odd,
A science project made by our dog.
Leftovers whisper, 'Eat me, I dare!'
But who needs yummies when dreams fill the air?

The couch, a kingdom of chips and crumbs,
Where we battled the TV and lost to the drums.
We laughed at the bloopers, cried at the memes,
Crashing like ninjas in inflatable dreams.

A closet splattered with shoes that don't fit,
Each one a tale, a memory, a skit.
In this strange house, where chaos ensues,
We sprinkle our lives with laughter's sweet hues.

The Attic of Wishes

Up in the attic, where dust bunnies play,
Ghosts of my dreams gather dust every day.
There's a bike I once rode, two wheels and a grin,
But now it's a throne for a rat with a kin.

Old photos of parties with hairstyles bizarre,
Even a cassette of my first rock star.
The echoes of laughter, the relics of pride,
Just need a good polish and maybe some tide.

Down from the rafters, a jump rope unfurls,
A time machine tethered to flip-skirted girls.
We'd leap into laughter, loop after loop,
Making jumps that now seem an impossible scoop.

The attic's a circus, a playground of want,
With laughter and dreams and a jester to flaunt.
I brush off the cobwebs, glimpse what's remained,
In this attic of wishes, my joy is sustained.

Spaces Unseen

Behind the door, surprises await,
A sock-taming monster and an old rubber mate.
We dance in the hallways, a quirky parade,
Each corner a riot, a joke to invade.

The laundry room's laughter, where colors collide,
I lost my dignity, but found socks with pride.
With every spin cycle, they giggle and sway,
As my mismatched adventures lead me astray.

The hallway may echo, but never stays still,
Crackling with laughter, it jumps with goodwill.
Each creak and each groan, a secret to share,
With walls that can whisper and spirits that care.

In these spaces unseen, where chaos resides,
We navigate life as the laughter abides.
With swirling confetti and quirks all in tow,
We flourish with joy in the spaces we know.

Joy and Pain Reside

In the living room, laughter paints walls,
But hidden behind it, silence gently calls.
Crack a joke, hear the chuckles arise,
Yet lurking beneath are tear-filled goodbyes.

The kitchen's a stage, where meals turn to fun,
Stirring up chaos 'til the bubbling's done.
We feast on the leftovers with giggles galore,
Ignoring the kitchen's big 'oops' on the floor.

In bedrooms, we dream, both silly and grand,
Building a world that we'll never quite land.
With pillows as clouds and blankets as seas,
We sail through the laughter, it flows like a breeze.

Through joy and through pain, we mesh and we blend,
In life's wacky journey, both foes and best friend.
With laughter as armor and love as our guide,
We dance through the seasons where joy and pain reside.

Lanterns in the Dark

In the attic, dust bunnies dance,
With old lamps that won't take a chance.
They flicker and waltz with a funny face,
Who knew they'd throw such a wild mix-up trace?

The laundry room's a spinning spree,
Where socks rebel, and tumble free.
The dryer claims a sock or two,
A sock thief's laughter rings right through!

In the kitchen, pots sing a tune,
With spatulas flying 'neath the moon.
Fridge magnets giggle in their place,
While leftovers plot their daring escape!

The bathroom mirrors whisper and shush,
As toothpaste dreams in a minty rush.
Shampoo bottles hold secrets tight,
While rubber ducks join the bedtime fright!

Fragments of Light

Under the bed, shadows hold a grudge,
With monsters arguing; it's a bit of a fudge.
They want to tickle the toes of the brave,
But giggles escape, and they can't misbehave.

In the hallway, echoes dance around,
Footsteps of cats on the prowl abound.
Each corner whispers a comedic tale,
Of heroic leaps that never prevail.

The closet hides costumes from times gone by,
With capes and hats for a dashing fly.
A superhero lost in a world of clothes,
Spinning tales of adventures, who knows?

The living room sprawls with cushions galore,
A fortress of fluff that always implores.
Pillow fights break out without a care,
As laughter erupts in the soft, static air!

Timeless Thresholds

Each door creaks with stories untold,
Of prankster children, daring and bold.
Sneaking through halls with laughter and cheer,
Every twist, every turn, bringing joy near.

Stairs have their squeaks, like a song on repeat,
Each stair is a joke, a mischievous feat.
They groan underweight, like they're in on the fun,
While racing to catch up with evening's run.

The front porch swings, a creaky delight,
Holding secrets of neighbors, gossip takes flight.
When shadows stretch long, and the sun starts to fade,
Gossiping ghosts come out, unafraid!

A window opens, the breeze is a tease,
Whispering stories in playful degrees.
And curtains flutter like they're in a parade,
Celebrating the chaos that life has made!

The Comfort of Shadows

By the fireplace, shadows dance and prance,
With flickering flames, they take a chance.
They waltz across walls, a grand charade,
In a darkening room, their fun displayed.

Books stack up high, each a playful plot,
Of quirky characters, giving a shot.
They argue and laugh, spilling ink on the floor,
Creating a mess that they just adore!

Cups of cold coffee hold stories to share,
With every sip, a memory laid bare.
The table's a throne for crumbs and spilled tea,
A banquet of laughter, just for me!

Outside the window, the stars wink and nod,
Inviting my thoughts to dance like a facade.
In the comfort of shadows, I find my delight,
As life plays its jests until the last light.

Reflections in Quiet Spaces

In the corner, a sock stands alone,
Once a pair, now a mystery grown.
Dust bunnies dance like they own the place,
While I trip on the carpet, a farcical grace.

A chair with a story, a squeak when I sit,
Dramatic moments, but no one to admit.
The fridge hums a tune, an off-key delight,
As my leftovers plot their escape in the night.

Cups stacked high, a teetering tower,
The coffee's gone cold, oh it used to empower.
A mirror reflects the day's goofy face,
Making notes of this strange, comical space.

Here in this bubble where the laughter is free,
The echoes of joy, just the fridge and me.
In my quiet corners, it's chaos on cue,
But I wouldn't trade this for anything new.

Tapestry of Time

A calendar marked with pizza night spree,
Each date a patch in my fabric, you see.
Stains from the sauce, a colorful blend,
This tapestry of time, where chaos won't end.

My couch is an island, lost in a sea,
Of crumbs and old shows, oh what a decree!
I search for the remote, like a treasure hunt,
Only to find it wedged in a laundry front.

Walls echo laughter from late-night debates,
Who eats the last slice? And who seals the fates?
With pillow fort battles, a knight without fear,
In this charming mess, all my friends gather near.

Each little mishap, a story retold,
In the fabric of fun, I find memories gold.
So I stitch and I sew these moments in rhyme,
In this quilt of existence, laughter's the prime.

Soft Light, Harsh Truths

Soft light filters in through a crack in the shade,
Bringing warmth to the mess that I've carefully made.
A pile of old clothes, a crumpled embrace,
Each wrinkle a memory that time can't erase.

The cat surveys all with a judging yum,
As if every dust mote is a hit to my crumb.
She watches my chaos with eyes of disdain,
While I tiptoe around to avoid her domain.

The alarm clock rings, it's too soon to be straight,
A battle with snooze, oh the temptress of fate!
Soft light plays tricks, could it really be noon?
As I linger in dreams, sipping from life's cartoon.

Harsh truths lay waiting in the laundry's loud call,
Mount Washmore is forming, it's about to enthrall.
But soft light whispering makes the worry retreat,
Laughter is freedom, under this cozy cheat.

Items Left Behind

Old shoes in the hallway, a puzzling affair,
Why do they linger, just hanging in air?
With soles full of stories, they've seen better days,
Yet here they reside, in a blurry malaise.

The remote on the couch, like a mythical beast,
Lost and forgotten, inviting a feast.
Every button a legend in this cushiony land,
Where the snacks have declared independence, unplanned.

A mug with a chip, a relic of tea,
In a battle of cups, it stands bravely, you see.
Rugged, determined, with stories galore,
It sips from the memories, ever wanting more.

Each item narrates a quirky old tale,
Of mishaps and laughter, the fun never pale.
Left behind treasures in my cluttered swirl,
In this enchanted space, my heart gives a twirl.

The Canvas of My Thoughts

In a corner, a sock does hide,
Its partner long gone, what a ride.
A pillow fights dreams through the night,
While crumbs laugh at the morning light.

The coffee pot sings, 'Fill me up!'
As the cat plans a cereal cup.
My plans fall like leaves in the breeze,
Laughter echoes and then it flees.

Old photos dangle, startled and shy,
Of bad hair days and a pie in the sky.
A dance with the dust, I oblige the floor,
With each step I trip, then I dance some more.

These walls hold secrets, funny and bright,
Where echoes of laughter burst into flight.
Maybe they're just losing their paint,
But they seem like the best kind of quaint.

Heartbeats Beneath the Ceiling

Under this ceiling, my jokes hit the fan,
The light bulb flickers, oh what a plan!
Shadows dance like they're late for a show,
While I search for snacks, taking it slow.

The clock ticks like it's in a rush,
While I wrestle my phone, in a digital crush.
The echo of laughter just cracks me up,
As the lamp shakes its head in a whimsical sup.

Whiskers on display, the cat strikes a pose,
While I trip on my shoes and land on my toes.
These heartbeats, they tickle the air quite a bit,
Making life feel like a colorful skit.

So here I reside with quirks and delight,
Each scene a twist, comedy in sight.
If only my neighbors could see what I see,
They might just call up a talk-show for me!

Portraits of Past Days

Pictures hung crooked, just like my style,
Each frame tells a tale, just wait a while.
An awkward pose here, a laugh caught mid-sneeze,
Remind me why I thought that looked like a breeze?

Oh, the dances I've had with my vacuum cleaner,
It pulls all my hair out, what a meaner!
With dust bunnies laughing, they scatter and roam,
Making my vacuum feel less like a home.

Beneath the world map, my dreams take flight,
Planning vacations, but the couch feels right.
A suitcase so dusty, it hides in despair,
While my passport dreams of fresh salty air.

Yet here in my gallery, I still dare to smile,
Amidst the portraits that sit in a pile.
Each memory a brushstroke, a giggle, a sigh,
A masterpiece crafted, oh me, oh my!

An Odyssey Through Four Walls

In my fortress, a kingdom of chaos and cheer,
Wearing mismatched socks is my greatest frontier.
A couch potato knight with a cape of potato chips,
Defending my kingdom with lazy quips.

The fridge stands guard, a soldier so proud,
With leftovers whispering, 'We're not allowed!'
Each shelf holds a story, both tasty and stale,
As I raid it like treasure, set out to unveil.

From the bathroom serenade to the laundry croon,
I perform my grand show, an off-key cartoon.
The walls seem to giggle, they get all the jokes,
As I prance like a fool, and the ceiling just pokes.

Yet beneath this roof, where the quirky reside,
I find joy and laughter, with wit as my guide.
Each wall stands a friend, each corner a chuckle,
In this funny adventure, life's just a cuddle.

Spaces where Love Lingered

In the corner, dust bunnies dance,
Whispering secrets of a lost romance.
A chair that squeaks with each sweet sigh,
Wonders how long until the next goodbye.

Under the table, a cat makes its bed,
Dreams of the crumbs we both never fed.
A fridge that hums a soft serenade,
Giving life to meals that were poorly made.

The walls have ears, they giggle and tease,
Recalling our laughter and awkward freeze.
The light bulb flickers like a nervous heart,
It knows our stories, our silly start.

So here we reside, in our quirky space,
Where love lingers on, with a funny face.
Each moment a memory, bright or absurd,
In the spaces between, love's whispers are heard.

The Diary of a Silent Room

A chair with a tale of a long, lazy day,
Recalls all the things we forgot to say.
Post-it notes linger, a rainbow of dreams,
With reminders of quests and old ice cream themes.

The dusty old clock sports a grin on its face,
It knows every tick is a wild, funny race.
Spider webs spin like a written scroll,
Telling of hiccups that took quite a toll.

The mirror reflects a belted-out tune,
Of hairbrushes singing to the glow of the moon.
With socks on the floor, a colorful fight,
Who knew that chaos could feel so right?

In the silent retreat where my thoughts often bloom,
Life scribbles its magic in every room.
And laughter is written in letters so bold,
In the diary of silence, funny tales unfold.

A Journey in Starlight

In twilight's embrace, socks start to stray,
Journeying across the floor, come what may.
Under the covers, the whispers take flight,
Guiding the dreams through the velvety night.

With popcorn crumbs mapping our starlit way,
And cushions that cushion our laughter's display.
A spaceship built out of blankets and cheer,
Zooms through galaxies of giggles and beer.

The moonlight checkmates the shadowy game,
Where giggles and antics never feel lame.
In starry-eyed visions, we dance and we weave,
Through the pathways of dreams that we gleefully leave.

So come, take a seat in this playful embrace,
And let starlight guide us to our happy place.
For in every laugh, and each silly plight,
We journey together, dancing in starlight.

The Gathering of Forgotten Echoes

In a nook of the past, they chuckle and sway,
The echoes of laughter from a far-off day.
A whoopee cushion sits with pride on the chair,
As memories bubble, giggles fill the air.

The moving boxes, they cheer in delight,
Recalling the chaos of packing at night.
Mismatched socks laugh at the game we once played,
While the dust gathers tales of the chaos we made.

The walls creak with stories, both silly and sweet,
Of dance moves performed in the middle of heat.
Old lamps sway like old friends in a rumba,
Casting light on the antics of our silly slumber.

So here they convene, the echoes long missed,
In the gathering place where the laughter insists.
A party of memories, they sing and they beam,
In the heart of a home built on joy's wild dream.

Chandeliers of Choice

In every corner, bright lights gleam,
The choice of colors makes it a dream.
I flipped the switches, oh what a sight,
They're flickering like they're dancing all night.

A chandelier made of odd knickknacks,
One from a yard sale, one from the racks.
I wonder if they whisper at night,
Trading secrets, oh what a delight!

The glow of decisions, hanging by threads,
Highlighting paths, where no one treads.
Some are flashy, others quite plain,
But all of them chat when I'm feeling insane.

So here's to the choices, bold and bright,
Illuminated wonders, a quirky sight.
In my vibrant space, laughter resides,
Under chandeliers of choices that guide.

Where the Heart Resides

In a cozy nook where laughter spills,
I chase my dreams, stack up my thrills.
With socks on the ceiling, and books on the floor,
My heart has found joy while I rummage for more.

The couch is a ship, sailing through time,
With snacks for the crew, oh how sublime!
Each cushion a wave, each pillow a port,
On this vessel of chaos, I'll never fall short.

Windows are portals to worlds far and wide,
Where laughter plays hide and seek, I'll confide.
Napping like royalty in fluffy delight,
Dreams bloom like flowers, colorful and bright.

So here in this haven, chuckles abide,
Where windowpanes frame the joy inside.
My heart finds a home in this playful spree,
In every tiny corner, wild and free.

The Space Between Us

In a tight little nook, we giggle and squish,
Fighting for room—oh, what a wild wish!
We share popcorn while dodging the crumbs,
In this space of laughter, joy softly hums.

The couch is a map, with cushions as hills,
Tales of our journeys give us the thrills.
A foot on my lap, an arm in my face,
Yet here in the mess, we've conquered this place.

Our bickering banter was once taken serious,
Now it's a dance, quite mischievous.
We throw pillows like poets toss rhymes,
In this space between us, laughter climbs.

So cheers to the clutter, the chaos, the fun,
Where space may be tight, but our joy's never done.
In the little gaps, we find all the good,
In the space that we share, we always understood.

Dusty Corners

In dusty corners where shadows thrive,
I discovered a treasure, oh my, what a hive!
Old toys are grinning, a relic parade,
In this time capsule, memories cascade.

Cobwebs dance like the stars on a night,
They weave tales of childhood, full of delight.
A dinosaur roars under a heap of old hats,
While a tattered teddy just sits, and chats.

With each dust bunny caught in a grin,
They whisper of stories and mischief within.
Grandpa's old shoes in a corner they stay,
As if waiting for someone to come out and play.

So I dive into layers, a curious find,
Each dusty corner a treasure, unlined.
In forgotten places, laughter still clings,
In these quirky alcoves, nostalgia sings.

Bright Futures

Reaching for dreams on glittering beams,
I scribble my hopes, oh how they gleam!
Each crayon drawing hangs like a star,
In my gallery of whimsy, I'll go far.

With laughter as paint, I color my way,
Through futures so bright, come what may.
A rainbow of wishes sprawls on my wall,
Each scribbled promise stands proud and tall.

I spin around in this colorful mess,
Embracing the chaos, I must confess.
In the dance of the colors, joy is my creed,
In every bright stroke, I plant a new seed.

So here's to the future with crayons galore,
Where laughter ignites and dreams start to soar.
In this vibrant canvas, my heart takes flight,
With shades of tomorrow, splashed in delight!

Corners Filled with Echoes

In every corner, laughter blooms,
Chasing shadows, it chases brooms.
Socks on the floor, a game we play,
Who stole the cookies? Oh, not today!

Chairs that creak, they sing a tune,
Whispers float like a weather balloon.
Pictures watching, they roll their eyes,
As a cat plots its great disguise.

The fridge hums a catchy beat,
As I waltz with the leftover meat.
In the madness, I find delight,
It's a circus show, by fridge light!

Echoes of giggles along the wall,
When the impromptu shows start to call.
I slip on a banana, what a sight,
In my own sitcom, I'm the highlight!

A Mosaic of Moments

Pieces scattered, smiles and sighs,
Sticky notes fly like butterflies.
Coffee stains form a master plan,
While I pretend to be the man.

Puzzles half-finished on the floor,
Every missing piece is a door.
A sock puppet speaks in silly tones,
As I ponder the joy of groans.

Kitchen chaos, a flour fight,
The aftermath, a snowy sight.
I twirl and slide, socks on the ground,
Making sure giggles are around.

In a whirlwind of joy and cheer,
Moments slice through like a spear.
With every mishap, a lesson learned,
In this mosaic, laughter is earned!

Veils of Solitude

Behind the curtain, a world unfolds,
Where socks are rebels, and chaos molds.
Cups of tea whisper secrets shy,
While I twirl with a sly butterfly.

The closet knows my deepest fears,
It swallows socks, it swallows tears.
As I talk to the dust bunnies so bold,
They give me wisdom, stories untold.

The bathroom mirrors crack a grin,
Reflecting the madness held within.
I dance with the shampoo, spinning 'round,
In veils of solitude, laughter found.

Every little creak carries a tale,
Of late-night snacks and grand fail.
In my haven, the world feels so bright,
Where solitude wears a crown of light!

Southern Exposure

Sunshine streams through the screen door,
Bugs join the dance on the kitchen floor.
Sweet tea spills like a gossip spread,
While I nap on a pillow of bread.

The hammock sways, it's a gentle ride,
As I ponder life with a side of pride.
The rooster crows, it's way past noon,
Got lost in dreams, softly crooning a tune.

Fireflies blink like tiny stars,
I try to catch them in empty jars.
The neighbors laugh, they're never shy,
With jokes that roll like a southern pie.

Picnics turn into grand soirées,
Melons and laughter, oh what a craze!
In the southern sun, we'll always bask,
In moments of joy, there's no need to ask!

Windows to My Soul

Through glassy panes I always stare,
Reflecting thoughts beyond compare.
I catch my friends in silly poses,
Making faces, striking noses.

Sunlight tickles my chin and cheek,
While outside, kids play hide and seek.
Birds flap by with chatter loud,
They're part of my goofy crowd.

Leaves tap dance upon the sill,
As if they're trying to make me chill.
I sip my tea with laughter bright,
And clink my cup to pigeon flight.

So when you peek and see me grin,
Know my shenanigans begin.
These windows show my playful quest,
A wacky heart that loves the jest.

The Colorful Walls of Me

My walls are draped in vibrant hue,
With splashes bold of pink and blue.
Polka dots dance in merry rows,
Inviting laughter as it flows.

There's a mural of my past mishaps,
Like losing socks and funny naps.
Each brushstroke tells a tale so grand,
Of cake fights that got out of hand.

A splash of green for nature's tease,
And orange zest to bring me ease.
These colors giggle day and night,
Creating joy, a true delight.

So walk inside and let it be,
A gallery of all that's free.
With every shade, a smile grows,
Capturing each hilarious pose.

Doors Unlatched

Each door I open squeaks a tune,
A symphony of laughs by noon.
From kitchen to the bathroom spree,
Where rubber ducks make melodies.

The front door welcomes with a wink,
As if it knows what I might think.
It swings and sways like it's alive,
Pulling me in for playful jive.

What lies beyond the closet space?
A treasure chest of socks misplaced.
Or maybe ghosts of shooed-out shoes,
That dance with dust and silly blues.

So, swing them wide and hear the cheer,
For every enter's full of dear.
These unlatched doors of joy untold,
A comedy that never gets old.

Whispering Hallways

In every hallway, secrets creep,
With echoes soft, they make me leap.
They giggle low and share a tease,
About my clumsiness with these.

There's a corner where I often trip,
A friendship formed through every slip.
The walls are quick to offer aid,
As I recover from my parade.

Pictures hang with cheeky grins,
They know the tales of all my sins.
They whisper loud when I pass by,
"Remember when you kissed that pie?"

So stroll these halls and hear the tales,
Of all my quirks and funny fails.
With every step, a laugh unfolds,
In corridors where life is bold.

The Fireplace of Reflection

In the corner, a chair sat,
A cat claimed it like a diplomat.
Logs crackled, a show so bright,
My thoughts danced in the soft twilight.

Marshmallows on a roasting stick,
Oh, how time can play a trick!
Though I ponder life with might,
I end up laughing at my plight.

From the flames, shadows will play,
Twisting stories in a sway.
Each flicker tells a jesting tale,
Embers wink as worries pale.

So gather 'round, let laughter swell,
With memories both sweet and swell.
In this cozy glow, I'll confide,
Life's a jigsaw, let's enjoy the ride!

Portraits in Time

On the wall, a face in a frame,
With a hat that brings a sense of fame.
My uncle's dapper, oh so slick,
One glance at him—it's quite the trick!

Grandma's photo, a mischievous grin,
A reminder of the fun within.
"Who wore it better?" we all debate,
In the gallery of our family fate.

Each portrait captures a silly scene,
Dressed in shades of bright and green.
Through laughter, our stories unfold,
These frozen moments never grow old.

As we gather, looking back,
With jokes and jibes, we'll never lack.
The canvas of life is multi-hued,
In this gallery, joy is renewed!

The Serenity of Stillness

A rocking chair sways, back and forth,
The cat snorts; he claims his worth.
A stillness falls, but watch the dust,
In quiet corners, giggles rust.

Birds outside compete with cheer,
"Can you be quiet, you ragged dear?"
While nature offers this silent song,
Inside, laughter can't stay strong.

The clock ticks loudly, mocking me,
As I muse on life's sweet irony.
In stillness, thoughts race at a spree,
While my cup of tea silently agrees.

So here I twiddle my thumbs in peace,
Yet jokes and jests refuse to cease.
Serenity's mockery is quite a thrill,
In silence, comedy fits the bill!

Chasing Sunbeams

In the garden, I spot a ray,
Sunbeams flicker, come out and play.
I run and leap like a bouncing ball,
As shadows giggle, I trip and fall.

Through the flowers, my laughter rang,
While the neighbor's cat began to hang.
"Are you chasing something too?" I muse,
But he only poses, refusing to choose.

Butterflies dance, thinking it's a game,
As I reach but they never tame.
"Catch me if you can!" they tease in flight,
While I tumble in laughter, what a sight!

So here I chase, beneath the blue,
Sunbeams and giggles, it's joy anew.
Life's a playground, so wild and free,
In every moment, just let it be!

Voices in Empty Rooms

In the hallway, echoes laugh,
Telling secrets of the past.
The lamps are winking, quite the jest,
They know just how I feel outclassed.

Chairs gossip when I'm not around,
Whispering tales of lost and found.
The fridge hums a silly tune,
It's the life of the party, who knew?

A picture frame rolls its eyes,
At the cat who swears she flies.
Socks in the drawer, a fashion show,
Did they really think I wouldn't know?

When footsteps patter, they make a dance,
In this space, where quirks enhance.
The dust bunnies chuckle, take a bow,
As I trip over shoes—I'll show 'em how!

The Footfalls of Time

Tick-tock, the clock's a tease,
It laughs at my forgetful keys.
Footsteps echo, a puzzling sound,
Is that me or the ghost? Who's around?

I swear the sofa's got a grin,
With each snack, it pulls me in.
Cushions whisper, 'Take a break!'
While I try to find what's at stake.

Brooms in the corner, they grumble and moan,
I swear they'd rather not be alone.
Dust settles in corners, perfectly poised,
While I act like there's nothing to avoid.

As time tiptoes and trips, I nod,
In this dance, I'm a little flawed.
Laughter weaves through each clumsy crime,
In grand choreography, I beat 'til prime.

Safe Havens

This cozy nook, my fortress grand,
A realm where no chores are planned.
The blanket fort stands tall and proud,
Telling the world to hush and bow.

The couch, my confidant, full of dreams,
Hiding snacks in its seams.
The cushions clutch stories untold,
In every fold, adventures unfold.

A secret drawer, my treasure trove,
Filled with memories and stickers to strove.
Each item whispers, 'Stay awhile,'
As I wrap up in warmth and style.

This hideaway, where giggles ring,
And laughter dances, what joy it brings.
In corners, I'll gather my peace of mind,
In this world of quirks, solace I find.

A Gallery of Grief

Painted walls with a hue of sighs,
Frames capture love, where laughter lies.
Yet in the silence, colors blend,
And memories loop, they twist and bend.

Each shadow dances, a familiar face,
A canvas of time, a mingled space.
The chair remembers every gaffe,
As ghostly giggles round the half.

My heart, a gallery, hung with the past,
Reminders that joy can shimmer fast.
As laughter echoes, each tear we trace,
In a funny dance, we find our place.

So here's to the art of laughing through,
In every corner, a spark we strew.
For grief and joy wear the same bright guise,
In this odd gallery, love never dies.

The Secrets We Store

In a closet of socks, mismatched and bright,
An army of dust bunnies battles each night.
The skeletons giggle behind the old chairs,
While the memories linger like forgotten affairs.

Old trophies stand tall, winners long gone,
And the smell of old takeout lingers on strong.
A stuffed owl perched high, watching with glee,
Hiding the snacks from both you and me.

Last week's dirty laundry sings out a tune,
Dancing with underwear, they'd make quite a boon!
Sudden surprises when I unlock that chest,
What was once garbage? Maybe it's the best!

With secrets and treasures piled up in a heap,
I wonder how long these wonders can keep.
Each corner holds laughter, quirks in their glow,
In this baffling maze, I'm never alone.

An Attic of Dreams

Up in the attic, where shadows conspire,
I found my old tricycle, a relic of fire.
Battered and bruised, still bright as a star,
It whispers of childhood adventures bizarre.

Boxes of knickknacks with stories to tell,
Like a soap opera set where oddities dwell.
There's a mirror that giggles and shows me my hair,
Reflecting a princess with a crown made of flare.

Dust motes are dancing like confetti in space,
As I try on hats from a time lost in grace.
A fortune-telling turtle with wisdom untold,
Predicts I'll eat pizza—a sight to behold!

So here in the clutter, I laugh and I dream,
Of dragons and castles, all fluffy and cream.
In this light-hearted haven, I dance and I sway,
In my attic of dreams, I'll forever play.

Halls of Longing

In the hallway, echoes of yesteryears roam,
With footsteps that stumble, they're far from home.
A picture of me in a dance long forgot,
Spinning in circles, giving it all that I've got.

Each door a reminder of wishes unmet,
With hidden regrets that I can't quite forget.
A cat on the stairs watches, quite wise,
As I trip over hopes that defy all the skies.

The fridge competes in its game of intent,
With leftovers plotting a zany event.
The light flickers on, casting shadows of cheer,
While the walls whisper secrets only I hear.

In this gallery of goofiness, I find my glee,
My heart beats in rhythm with unusual decree.
With a grin and a giggle, I gallivant through,
In the playful abyss where my dreams come true.

Paintings and Paradoxes

On the wall hangs a portrait of a cat wearing shoes,
Strutting with grace, with not a hint of blues.
A landscape of jelly on a plate full of cheese,
Composed in a moment, a sight meant to please.

A canvas of laughter that stretches so wide,
Where colors collide with nowhere to hide.
Each brushstroke a giggle, each daub holds a wish,
A banquet of nonsense on a whimsical dish.

Pondering art that's both splendid and strange,
With socks as my subjects, the tone starts to change.
The paradox tickles my heart with a tease,
In this wacky gallery, I muse with such ease.

The meanings are twisted like pretzels on sticks,
Where puzzles and riddles perform funny tricks.
In the merriment shared with each quirky design,
I find all the joy in these pictures of mine.

www.ingramcontent.com/pod-product-compliance
Lightning Source LLC
Chambersburg PA
CBHW062110280426
43661CB00086B/402